IN THE BEGINNING GOD

CREATED

BRIDGING THE GAP BETWEEN
ART AND YOUR CREATOR

Created: Bridging the Gap between Your Art and Your Creator

Published by Likable Art, 2017
Fort Wayne, Indiana, USA

This book is dedicated to the next generation of artists.
The future of the culture lies in your hands.
The perception of the Church is yours to mold.

This book is dedicated to Tyler Peltier: a friend, a hero, and a trailblazer.

This book is dedicated to my wife Marie, who shows me the world in color.
This book is dedicated to Henry, Fulton, and Pio.
Boys: You can do all things through Christ who strengthens you.

IN THE BEGINNING GOD CREATED

Genesis 1:1

These are the first five words that God decided to share with humanity.
Take a moment and let that sink in.

It sunk in for me a couple of years ago. For some reason, when my eyes crossed those words, they struck me anew. They spoke to my heart as a member of the artistic community.

Here is the weird and amazing reality for artists. Every time our pen hits the paper, every time we click the shutter, every time we lay the first brick, we share in that ultimate, lifegiving, unceasing action. Just like the moon reflects the sun, our little acts of creation reflect the moment that first Created us.

Artists. Makers. Tinkerers. Dreamers. Poets in every medium.
We are each Created, and we are in turn blessed to be creators.

Inspired by this thought, I went to the people that I look up to and asked them a simple question: "What are your first five words to the world of artists?"

And the responses came. Each one beautiful and moving in its own way, as diverse as the artists who shared them. With each one that popped into my inbox, I was moved further into the depths of God's overflowing heart. I think you will be as well.

CORY HEIMANN

LEAD · WITH

BEAUTY

There is something unthreatening about the beautiful, which is what makes it so powerful as a pathway to God: first the beautiful, then the good, and finally the true.

Consider a young man watching a skillfully played game of baseball. It awakens in him a profound desire to play like the players on the field. Then, once he begins himself, the actual playing of the game teaches him, from the inside, the rules and rhythms of baseball. It would be completely inadequate to draw a kid into the world of baseball by starting with a clarification of the rules or with a set of drills. Rather, we need to show him the beauty of baseball (the beautiful), so that he will want to play (the good), and having played, he will know how to play (the true).

I might suggest that Catholic creatives start with something like the Sistine Chapel or the life of Francis of Assisi, captivating even the most bored agnostic. Then allow that captivation to lead to a desire, perhaps vague at first, to participate in the moral universe that made those artistic expressions possible. Finally, the participation will conduce toward a true and experiential understanding of the thought patterns that undergird that way of life.

First the beautiful, then the good, then the true. That's the right pattern. Catholic creatives should lead with beauty.

BISHOP **ROBERT BARRON**

Auxiliary Bishop of the Archdiocese of Los Angeles
Founder of Word on Fire
wordonfire.org

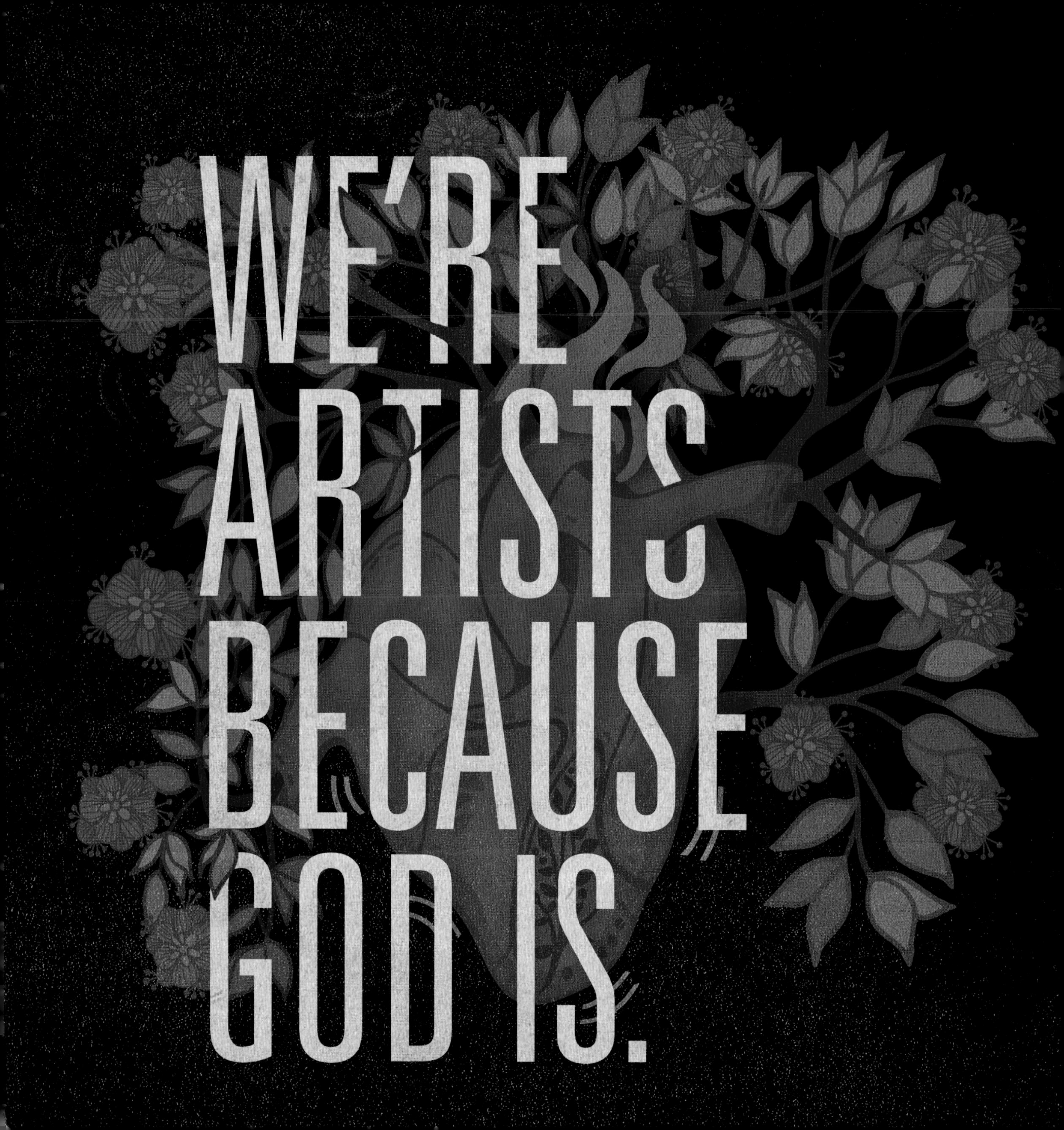
WE'RE ARTISTS BECAUSE GOD IS.

There's beauty everywhere. We just don't see it. Life is a mystery to be lived continuously, not a problem to be solved suddenly.

Everything that exists has some truth, some goodness, and some beauty. Everything is divine revelation. We are creators because we are created in the image of the Creator. We are artists because God is, and it's because we dimly know this that we weep with both joy and sorrow when we meet someone who pulls up the curtain an inch—the curtain that separates the heavenly vision from the earthly.

How do we use this to save the world? How do you appreciate beauty? You just love it. How do appreciate goodness? You just love it. How do you find the truth? You love it. Seek and you shall find. Truth, goodness, and beauty. You just do it. It's like, "How do you love? How do you pray? How do you live?" Just do it.

DOCTOR **PETER KREEFT**

Professor of Philosophy, Boston College
Author of over 75 books

BEAUTY
OFTEN GOES
UNSEEN

 Beauty is found everywhere, yet often it goes unseen.

While filming in the war-torn villages of Bosnia in 1993, I came to an area completely abandoned. Every home was empty. The only evidence of life in this town were the things fleeing families couldn't carry: burnt family photographs, broken furniture, and some children's toys left scattered in the rubble. It had become a ghost town.

Peering through my camera lens, I couldn't help but think about the generations of people who inhabited this area and how, in a fraction of a second, they were gone. This must have once been a peaceful place, and I wondered if it would ever again offer the serenity and life it once had.

As I put my camera down, something in the distance caught my eye. Amid wreckage and twisted metal, a single flower had found roots and raised its petals towards the sun.

I believe this is how God can speak to us, through nature's beauty, and on that day, it was as if He was saying: "I make all things new again." Revelation 21:5)

JOSEPH CAMPO

Filmmaker
Producer and Director at Grassroots Films, Inc.

INCREASE THE STOCK OF AVAILABLE REALITY

OK, that's six words and they may not exactly trip off the tongue but pause for a moment and just take them in. I stole those words from a book review I read once because they more or less blew my mind. The reviewer was speaking about how a book of poetry increased the stock of available reality.

T.S. Eliot once said: "Humankind cannot bear much reality." We know this is true. When it comes to the truth of the human condition, including our own dependency and need, we are like the proverbial ostrich. In any given historical epoch, how much reality is available to us? What sort of blinders do we put on?

Art exists to remove those blinders. The great film director Akira Kurosawa said: "The artist is the one who does not look away." At its best, art helps us to face not only darkness and evil but also the hiddenness and mystery of grace.

In our allegedly post-Christian time, one of the great things art can do for us is make available the reality of religious experience. Many people of faith have given into despair about our times and yet the work is out there, if we only look for it.

GREGORY WOLFE

Writer, Editor, and Publisher
Founder of *Image* | imagejournal.org
gregorywolfe.com

ART

OPENS

WINDOWS

TO

ETERNITY

In his *Letter to Artists*, St. John Paul II echoed Dostoyevsky's prophetic statement, "Beauty will save the world." Beauty will indeed save the world because beauty, and its artistic expressions, offers to the world the true vision of life, a sacramental-liturgical view of reality. This is true of the sacred art of the Church and, in particular, Byzantine iconography.

The ancient form of Byzantine iconography, to use a phrase from St. Augustine, is "so ancient yet so new." It is timeless. Iconography gives us a vision of the Great Mystery, the Incarnation. The truth of this life is that Heaven has touched earth. Therefore, the truth of all created things is that they reveal and indeed participate in God, most especially the human person.

Byzantine iconography incorporates the elements that make something beautiful—order, patterns, symmetry, balance, conscious and subconscious patterns, composition, color harmony, and above all, mystery.

Icons are a window into eternity, theology in color. Icons are also a mirror. Earth mirrors Heaven. The human person is made in the image and likeness of God. To see life through the vision of sacred art and to touch everything in life through that vision will indeed save the world.

FATHER **THOMAS J. LOYA** STB, MA

Pastor and Iconographer
byzantinecatholic.com

ARTISTS
CAN
HELP
REORIENT
EROS

Good art, especially the beauty of music, has always tapped a deep ache inside of me. While I felt that ache for (and from) beauty my whole life, I didn't know it was called *eros* until I stumbled upon Saint John Paul II's *Theology of the Body* in my early twenties. That erotic longing, I learned, defines us as creatures who hunger for God.

In lectures around the world, I've asked countless thousands this question: How many of you would say that in your Christian upbringing there was open, honest, healthy conversation about God's glorious plan for erotic longing? Consistently, I get about a 1-2% response. The other 98% of us were raised on what I call the "starvation diet gospel." We hear the rules, and they may well be true, but truth holds no appeal when it's cut off from our yearning for beauty. In turn, like an unfed dog, our hunger can become ravenous.

If we're prone to scorn truth without beauty, we're also prone to porn beauty without truth, fixating ourselves on idealized and hyper-eroticized images of beauty for the sake of a selfish, base gratification. When this is our approach to feeding *eros*, we're forfeiting the divine banquet and settling for "fast food." Today the Church desperately needs artists whose work flows from the ache of a properly oriented *eros*, an *eros* that can help lead others to Infinity ... and beyond!

CHRISTOPHER WEST

Author and Speaker
Fill These Hearts: God, Sex, & the Universal Longing
www.corproject.com

"Beauty has always been a natural stimulus to transcendence. Art can provide a feast for the senses that allows mankind to get a foretaste of the heavenly banquet. Continued gazes at beauty elevates and helps to set one free from the chains of the lesser loves that the world has to offer.

With the positive implications of exposure to such beauty, it should be of primary concern for the Church today to foster and nurture its creation.

The Incarnation of Christ sanctions the use of the visible form to mediate invisible truth. By creating, artists have the unique opportunity to participate in the work of Christ, bringing to flesh expressions of God's love and mercy.

Artists, Christ has invited you to create. Use the power of beauty to reveal, to transform, and to fall in love."

JOE KIM

Designer and Creative Director
PAL Campaign
palcampaign.com

Math is for Makers.

 Math is everywhere in the natural world, from the fractal shapes of leaves, clouds, and shorelines, to the beautiful, crystalline structure of snowflakes. But have you ever stopped to wonder if God has something to say to us through math?

Science says that the Creator of the Universe accomplished His work with a Big Bang - an impulse containing all of space and time, and all of nature still resonates with its power. The math that put the stars and the planets perfectly in place came from *that moment*. The math that caused the sun to be eclipsed at the time and place where His Son was crucified...came from *that moment*.

In particular, we find math expressed in music. When I was a teacher, one of my favorite units to teach was the "Science of Sound". I can't say this was necessarily reciprocal, as evidenced by the complaints of my students. Before I lost them, I would ask this question: "How did God teach humans what music was?"

The answer is that the blueprint of music is found in every tonal sound. The architecture of a grand major chord is found in every vibration; not locked away, but perfectly accessible and waiting to be discovered. Music is really just applied math. The math isn't incredibly complex; rather, it's beautifully simple and elegant. Music was there from the very beginning – a path for every love song between the Bridegroom and His bride.

Music and math both reveal something of the nature of this Creator and how we are to respond. For something to be beautiful, it must be ordered; it must be obedient. He is the conductor; we are the orchestra. This beautiful math provides the formula to orienting and surrendering your heart to your lover.

NATHAN PROULX

Music Technologist
nateproulx.com

Beauty will Save the World

Art isn't easy. An amateur artist, still stumbling and falling and producing inadequate initial works, is still an artist, albeit one who needs to throw himself more fully into the craft, to allow time to pass and canvases to be wasted and words to be deleted and songs to be discarded.

But like our sin-laden lives, sometimes in the midst of mediocre works of art, we see God's hand reaching through and sense within the working of our own hands, the guidance of the hand of God, pulling us through the muddled paint and cobbled together words and asynchronous chords to glimpse the potential placed within us by God Himself, who desires to share with us "something [akin to] the pathos with which God at the dawn of creation looked upon the work of his hands" (St. John Paul II, *Letter to Artists*).

As Dostoyevsky wrote, beauty will indeed save the world, but we as artists must be willing to stumble and crawl and seek the creative guidance of the Creator so as to bring forward the beauty that is His and His alone, even if through our own deficiencies. And it is through this beauty that the world will be drawn to Him. And by Him and His beauty, they will be saved.

GREG WILLITS

Author, Podcaster, and Artist
gregandjennifer.com

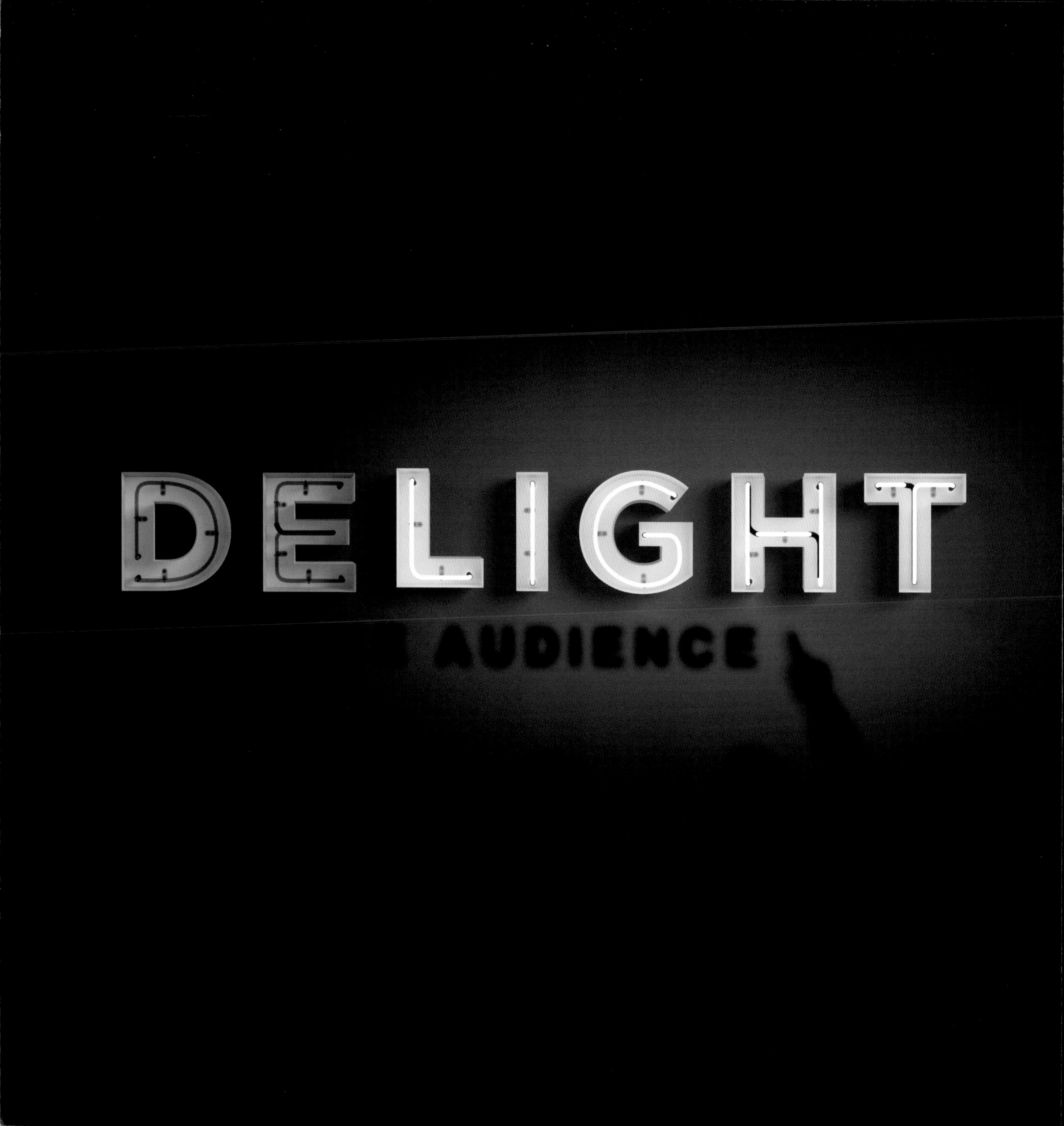
DELIGHT
AUDIENCE

That's what they taught us when I studied screenwriting at UCLA. How do we "only connect"? First, by loving our audience. If we love them and are creating for them (without pandering, but being true to our authentic impulses, insights, intuitions, and inspirations), they will feel that. If our art flops? It's always our fault. Chris Rock says that if the audience doesn't laugh, the *onus* is always on him. He wasn't funny.

Love people. But we artists are people, too. If it doesn't delight you, it won't delight others. If it doesn't make you laugh, it won't tickle anyone else's funny bone either. Write the movie you want to see. The personal is universal. The most specific is the most general.

Good actors instinctively create rapport with the audience. They signal that they are aware of us (in that way that only they can). Some actors are all caught up only in themselves and their craft, and we sense that, too. It's not really for us. They're closed off. Be a generous artist with the bountiful largesse of our Lord. We create for an A-list audience.

A wonderful motto for artists of any ilk is the motto of my congregation, the Daughters of St. Paul. It's the song of the Christmas angels: GLORIA DEO + PAX HOMINIBUS. All glory to God, yes. But don't forget His people.

SISTER **HELENA RAPHAEL BURNS** FSP

Speaker, Writer, and Filmmaker
mediaapostle.com

Flannery O'Connor once remarked: "I am not afraid that the book will be controversial; I am afraid it will *not* be controversial."

Like O'Connor, Christ was controversial. His parables occasionally depicted dramatic scenes involving violence and greed in order to reveal a higher truth: the reality of grace and the role of mercy in the sinful world of man. Christ challenged his audience. He overturned their tables. He dined with their rejects. He publicly denounced (Matthew 23) influential members of their community as "hypocrites" and "blind guides."

He told stories that challenged his audience:
to love more (Luke 10:25-37),
to give more (Mark 12:41-44),
to forgive more (Matthew 18:21-35).

Christ refused to let the fear of controversy diminish his ministry. He challenged his audience to use their God-given capacity for thought. He didn't follow "I desire mercy, not sacrifice" with a clear explanation of what that meant. Rather, he actually said: "Go and learn the meaning of the words, 'I desire mercy, not sacrifice'" (Matthew 9:13). He presented them with a paradigm-shifting truth, then challenged them to unpack it, accept it, and live it.

Does contemporary Christian art challenge us in that way? In my experience, rarely.

In the quest to understand what it means to be human in light of the divine, there are no heights without the depths. The depths will always be rife with controversy. Don't shy away from it. Don't fear it. Bring it to the light. Present it for discussion in your own uniquely creative way. To merely bask in the glory of the heights without ever diving into the depths is to remain comfortable. But, as Pope Benedict XVI said, "... you were not made for comfort. You were made for greatness".

KEVIN HEIDER

Musician
kevinheider.com

I hate New Years' Resolutions because, for me, it'll last for about 2 weeks (if I'm lucky), then I'll get bored, lazy, whatever, and move on.

Enter the year 2015.

I decided I wanted to create a concrete goal to practice my love of hand lettering and thus, The Oodles Of Doodles on Instagram was born.

The idea was to set aside at least 30 minutes a day for 365 days and doing a simple hand lettered/ watercolor quote and post it to Instagram for accountability. I figured, if I didn't have at least 30 minutes a day to do something I loved, then I was way too busy. I was creating pieces from an overflow of my prayer life... and people started following and noticing. Eventually the year ended, but I had fallen in love with this craft and had turned it into a beautiful little ministry.

We are not born with perfect gifts, but we CAN perfect our gifts to the best of our abilities. So practically speaking, spend at least 30 minutes a day perfecting or honing your craft. Do it because you've been given unique talents and gifts that only you have to collaborate with the Creative God.

ALI HOFFMAN

Hand Letterist
@theoodlesofdoodles on Instagram

> There it was. As I rounded the corner, I came face to face with one of the most famous paintings in the world, the *Mona Lisa.* As I worked through the crowd to approach the painting, I couldn't help but think of the many people who over the years had also experienced this work and been impacted by it.
>
> If your life were a painting, what would it look like? Would it be an impressionist piece in the style of Vincent Van Gogh, an abstract Jackson Pollock, or carry the intense dramatic tension found in Baroque classics? What color would it be? Would it be bright or dark, intricate or simple? Naturalistic or Surreal?
>
> Most of us can point to times in our lives where our painting has been ugly, and other times when it has been quite beautiful. It can be difficult to see the changes that take place day to day, but year over year the strokes layer over each other, creating fundamental changes to our work's composition. At our funeral, after the paint has dried, our masterwork is hung for all to see. The pews will fill and our loved ones will gaze at our casket, similar to the throngs of visitors that crowd around the Mona Lisa.
>
> Ultimately, the art we become is far more important than the art we create, and to create our masterwork, the Master must apprentice us.
>
> "I am confident of this, that the one who began a good work in you will continue to complete it until the day of Christ Jesus." Philippians 1:6

STEVEN LAWSON

Director of Communications at Dynamic Catholic
stevenvlawson.com

Quality

ISN'T

Expensive

IT'S

Priceless

It's no secret that we respond to quality. That's how businesses thrive. Yet, if we're honest, those words rarely describe our Church's efforts. (By Church, I include you and me.) If we observe people's experience of our Church, we'll see that often people aren't being moved by quality, rather they're tolerating mediocrity. That mediocrity comes with a cost.

Mediocrity drives people away. We may not intend it, but if we settle for it, mediocrity will give people a reason not to engage the Church. Mediocrity speaks, sometimes subconsciously, to the lack of investment and perceived worth of the people we are tasked to engage.

Still, we've largely become accustomed to sacrificing quality for the sake of expense. That's one of the problems: we see quality as an expense rather than an investment. When we view anything as merely an expense, it usually reduces the goal to simply getting the job done and leads to a mediocre result that is "good enough." However, when we see something as an investment, we face the cost with the mindset that it will pay off greatly down the line. This mindset frees us to operate according to a desired result rather than limiting what we do based upon saving a buck or two.

As Christians, we are called to invest into life. Jesus showed us what this investing looks like, he called it love. Love never holds back, never looks for the path of least resistance - or least expense. We see this on the cross, the totality of a quality and priceless love on display. We're called to image that love. This love demands that we strive for quality in the face of expense – be it time, money, or other – because God, the Gospel, and His people are with it.

DAVID CALAVITTA

Speaker and Designer
Head of Design and Marketing at Life Teen International
holdfasthope.com

PLay
&
PRaYer

GO TOGETHER

St. Thomas Aquinas proposed that play and prayer go together because both are done for their own sakes and the unintended fruit for both is joy.

God wants us to play.

We are to creatively play with our ideas, our actions, and our words, certainly not in any irresponsible sense, but as His children, trusting in Him, doing all for Our Lord's glory and the sanctification of souls.

The Word of God proclaims in the eighth chapter of Proverbs: "I was beside him as his craftsman, and I was his delight day by day, playing before him all the while, playing on the surface of his earth; and I found delight in the sons of men". Our Father, the divine Artist, with loving regard, passes on to each one of us a spark of His own surpassing wisdom, calling us, His kids, to share in His creative power, as St. John Paul II reminds us in his *Letter to Artists*. When we create with this worldview, a worldview that encompasses all human endeavors, we are better able to engage reality and express goodness and truth. We become custodians of beauty, and ultimately, we become more like Jesus, little children playing before Our Father.

DOCTOR **EUGENE GAN**

Professor at Franciscan University of Steubenville
Author, Speaker and Artist
eugenegan.weebly.com

QUANTITY THEN QUALITY

We hate wasting time. So we tend to move forward with a good idea or a solution to a problem quickly. But often, that good idea could be a great idea if we spent more time in the pre-planning.

Let me give you a simple example. If I'm designing a graphic, I might type out the text, and start scrolling through fonts. Usually this means trying dozens, if not hundreds, of fonts before finding the best one. I could stop on the first font that is good, or keep trying until I find the best font that I have, or even look for fonts I don't yet own. Once I find the right font, then I can mess with leading/kerning, size, weight, etc...

When writing music, I like to write as many demos as possible. In fact, one year, I tried writing a song-a-day and the goal was to record 100 demos. I did, and only a couple of those were finished and tweaked and recorded on our next CD.

Design is finding solutions to problems. So first, brainstorm on ideas, try things, experiment, start with quantity. Then, when you finally come up with the best idea, dig into that and spend quality time working on it.

I love the failures, the wrong fonts, the dumb songs, because I had to get that out of me to get to the good ones. You need to get out the bad ideas because those lead to good ideas. They are part of the journey.

Note: I probably had 30 different ideas for my "Five words" and I picked my favorite and worked on it. And the graphic over there, that is version 13. By the way, this was originally titled, "Failures are just success fetuses."

KYLE HEIMANN

Musician and Radio Host
Host of The Kyle Heimann Show
kyleheimann.com

crap man I'm not sure I can do it...also not sure I could make something good enough for the book....

I had an idea to print out like 30 different pictures of me from my Facebook profile from 2007-2017 and then creating a montage and painting the words "Honest before polished" on it.....but alas I doubt I would actually do it

ha

We can take care of it

although even a horrible swing at this one might fit the context perfectly

honestly I'm nervous I wouldn't make anything up to par with the book

which is in direct contradiction to what I wrote....but still...

exactly

I think I'm just going to screenshot this conversation and make that the design

7:47PM

that is beautiful on so many levels

BE honest BEFORE polished

type a message...

The world has seen centuries of artists, creators, inventors, writers, and makers. Why make or say anything? It's all been made or said before. Do we have within us anything novel enough or good enough to offer in the company of the giants of the past?

I believe we make stuff because we have something no one else can say. As kids, we learn to talk by reflexively repeating words. Then we start to choose the words we imitate. We say something small about ourselves: "I'm thirsty", "I'm hungry". But slowly, and with practice, we learn to combine lots of words to speak out of something deep within, something unique and unrepeatable.

If we practice self-awareness and are diligent in speaking only the truth, we can learn to communicate a word no one can know or speak but us, the word written on our heart - our very self. It's not easy, saying something honest. It is risky and usually comes with a cost. You'll be tempted to say something prettier. You'll be tempted to say something easier. You'll be tempted to be polished before you are honest. And that's when you'll lose what makes your art valuable.

"Man looks on the outward appearance, but the Lord looks on the heart."
1 Samuel 16:7

LETTERING: MARIE HEIMANN | fawnly.com

EDMUND MITCHELL

Maker
Founder of Reverb Culture and Lumibox
edmundmitchell.com

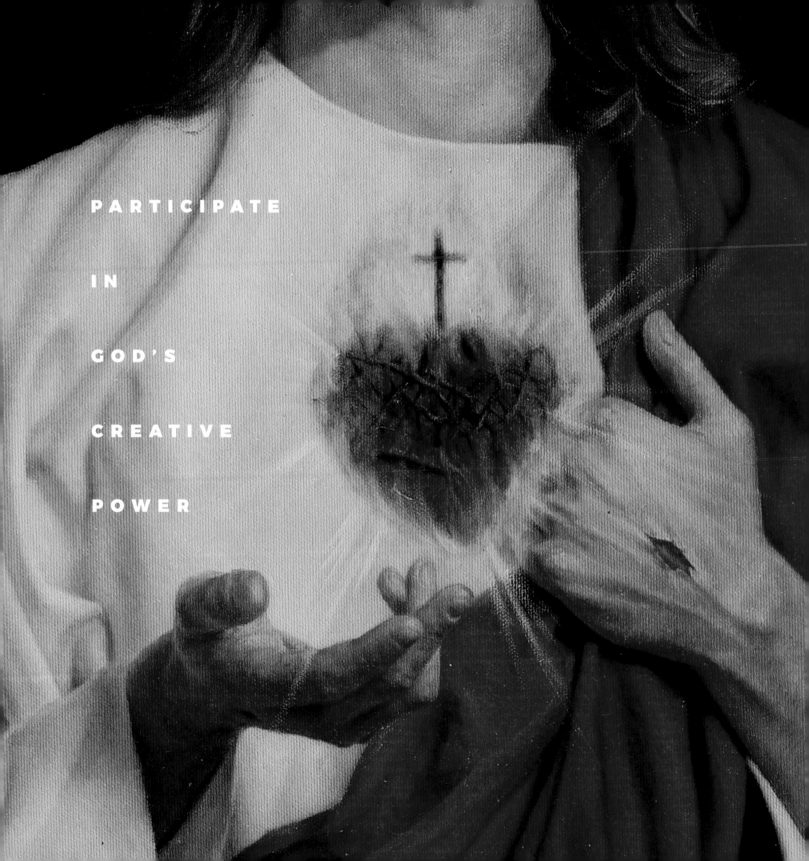

PARTICIPATE

IN

GOD'S

CREATIVE

POWER

I often admire and am amazed by God's creation, and always come to the conclusion that you cannot create something more beautiful than what God has created. In fact, I think it is impossible for us to truly create at all. Rather, man is called to participate in the creative power of God by way of procreation- a unique gift that we are given.

As artists, we ourselves are a work of art. We are the result of a relationship of love, an infinite and eternal love that the creative hands of God physically manifests through the bodies of our parents. It is amazing how life can be born from two humans, two small creatures of dust. The artist has the responsibility of living out his or her work as a true gift of love, as a result of a relationship with God. Through this effort, we can be a light for all humankind. We can sense the beauty that is present in our midst.

We do so only through God's grace, without making an effort to seek something "new" or artificial. Rather, we can learn to see the new and beautiful in what is present in our human nature, which is fragile and even suffering; yet elevated by the Son of God, who became man like us.

MARGHERITA GALLUCCI

Painter
margheritagallucci.com

YOUTH CULTURE *NEEDS* CATHOLIC ART

"When I was studying to become a youth minister, I was taught that you have seven minutes; only seven minutes to make your point before teenagers will lose focus - only seven minutes. Any longer and they may doze off and miss your point entirely.

It's not easy to captivate teens. Every business, clothing line, tv network, and pop singer in the world is fighting for seven minutes of their attention. As a church, I think we tend to shy away from that fight. We write of youth culture as faddish or shallow. We keep doing things "as we've always done them" and leave good design and talent to the Protestant churches.

The truth is youth culture needs Catholic art. Teens are hungry for art that doesn't just sell them a shirt, an album, or a cause to rally behind. They hunger for art that answers the deepest questions in their hearts. They want to be captivated by work that was labored over, that speaks to them; not just the opinion of another high and mighty artist, but the truth. They hunger for the truth of the Gospel.

That might require us as artists to rethink how we do things. It might require us to do research and evolve our style. It might take a lot of work. But if in those seven minutes, a teen meets Jesus through my work, I'd say it was all worth it.

RYAN MCQUADE

Graphic Designer at Life Teen

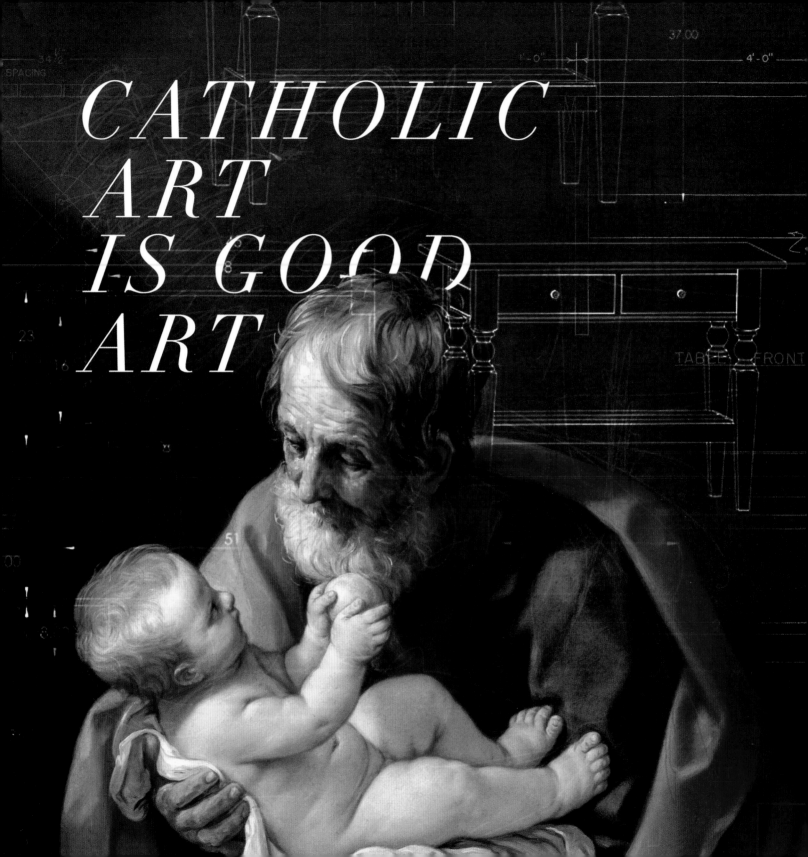

CATHOLIC ART IS GOOD ART

What did Jesus do during the first 30 years of his life? Think about it. That's a long time, three decades of "hiddenness" before his public ministry. How did he spend those days? Watching and working.

Who was he watching? Mary, of course. But he spent more time watching his father, Joseph, at work in the carpentry shop. He noted Joseph's precision—for he was a saint who wasn't sloppy—and his commitment to quality, refusing to submit half-baked work. Jesus absorbed those lessons. Then when he was old enough, he joined his father. Thus Jesus became a worker. And by working with wood, he was an artisan. And as an artisan, he was an artist.

Benches, tables, chairs, doors—all of that was made by Joseph's boy, and it must have been made well. It must have been good art. No "just good enough" art would have left that shop. As Dorothy Sayers notes, in her remarkable reflection on work:

"The Church's approach to an intelligent carpenter is usually confined to exhorting him not to be drunk and disorderly in his leisure hours, and to come to church on Sundays. What the Church should be telling him is this: that the very first demand that his religion makes upon him is that he should make good tables. Church by all means, and decent forms of amusement, certainly–but what use is all that if in the very center of his life and occupation he is insulting God with bad carpentry? No crooked table legs or ill-fitting drawers ever, I dare swear, came out of the carpenter's shop at Nazareth. Nor, if they did, could anyone believe that they were made by the same hand that made Heaven and earth. No piety in the worker will compensate for work that is not true to itself; for any work that is untrue to its own technique is a living lie."

Catholic art, to be worthy of the name, must be good art first. Joseph knew this. Jesus knew this. Catholic artists have known it, up and down the centuries.

Now it's our turn.

BRANDON VOGT

Author and Content Director at Word on Fire
Founder of ClaritasU
brandonvogt.com

ICONS ARE SERMONS IN COLOR

As Catholics, we have a rich heritage of great art. Because of artists like Giotto and Da Vinci and art like the Pieta and Sainte-Chapelle and so many others, the art of the Church has helped lift countless souls to God through its beauty. It is often through beauty that God speaks to the soul, and so it is often through the beauty of art that the Church preaches to the soul of man. Throughout history, the Church's mission has always been to preach the Gospel of salvation: to bring men to Jesus Christ and make them saints.

The lives of the saints who have gone before us (so often the subjects of Catholic art) are themselves a sermon, a collection of stories. The Church passes on these stories of wisdom, courage, grace, and perseverance through the medium of sacred art, a form of storytelling though symbols. Icons of saints feature items of a saint's life: books and quills for writers, lilies for virgins, and the instruments of their death for martyrs. Backgrounds of gold symbolize the radiance of heaven, and so forth.

Sacred art echoes the Church's message of reminding us of what our goal in this life is, namely, to become saints. As Léon Bloy once wrote: "The only real failure, the only great tragedy in life, is not to become a saint." Images of the saints encourage us to follow in their footsteps and inspire us to ask the saints to help us on our own path to sanctity. The saints are part of our family, and they're there to help cheer us on through the finish line. What an awesome thing it is to have one's artwork be an instrument of grace to help a person on the path to holiness!

CECILIA LAWRENCE

Iconographer, Pyrographer, and Painter

Why do you create? Beyond affirmation, accolade, fame or fortune...where does the fire within you come from to create something new? Where does that passion emanate from to allow your internal longings and movements to be manifest in external ways?

Why does one paint or sculpt?
Why does one write or sing?
Why does one compose or perform?

It's for the same reason that fish swim and birds fly...

Simply put, because we give glory to God by doing what we are designed to do. God is more than a Creator, He is a divine designer. Every facet of creation, every intricacy is an arrow pointing creation back to the Creator.

"The heavens are telling the glory of God; and the firmament proclaims his handiwork." Psalm 19:1

What is even more amazing is that you were created in Christ Jesus to do these good works (Ephesians 2:10)! You were not created just for creations' sake. You were designed for beauty's sake. Every time you draw on the creative gifts and talents entrusted to you to unleash beauty upon the world you glorify your Father.

So keep creating. Swim. Fly. It's what you were designed to do.

MARK HART

Author, Speaker, and Catholic Evangelist
Vice President of Life Teen International
lifeteen.com

EXPANSION,
FAR SURPASSING WHAT'S WORLDLY

Art must speak of beauty in union with truth and goodness. Yet, if an artist has not truly encountered these foundations, their work will be but noise or worse, deception. Catholic artists have a particular obligation to counteract the current, relativistic trends that claim truth to be subjective. As missionaries of beauty, they are entrusted with communicating mysteries that are well beyond social constructs and that stand on the solid foundation of truth, goodness, and beauty. Thus, in-order for an artist to rise to such a task, they must personally encounter these foundations and seek after an expansion that far surpasses what is worldly and fully encompasses one's senses, heart, mind, and skills.

This continual expansion begins at the feet of God in stillness. It is through this encounter with true Beauty Himself that one begins to perceive more fully his or her own being, the world, and the wonders they point to. From there, an artist is called to cultivate the talents given, thus, to seek an excellence that is married to these same foundations. Artists, may we imitate the Marian posture of openness and make time for the very expansion of our beings as well as our skills, crafting a *fiat* as our visible love song.

KATE CAPATO

Sacred Artist, Photographer, and Choreographer
visualgrace.org

At what point does an experience or interaction gain the title "spiritual" or "secular"? We describe a certain photograph of an Afghan woman staring hauntingly into the lens as "moving" – but what if the picture is hanging on the corner of a public library? What if it has no traditionally spiritual theme or title or description? How would we describe it to our friends?

I propose that everything is spiritual because God is truly present, moving, and active in all things. God isn't residing "up above" in Heaven as an abstract idea or a simply outdated and irrelevant creator; God is here. Every reaction, emotion, sunset, hug, painting, film, or word spoken has the potential to be a wealth of divine interaction. Goodness, beauty, and truth cannot only subsist in a painting of the Last Supper – it is anointed in our heart as an orientation towards God... how we interact, reflect, and discern the many experiences of the "secular" world depends on our willingness to enter authentically enter in.

DAN ROGERS

Filmmaker, Photographer, and Designer
Co-founder of Imagine Sister Movement
avenuecreativephx.com

LOVE IS THE ONLY SOLUTION

One thing we often forget as Catholics is that we are radically called to do everything in our lives in Christ, through Christ, with Christ, and for Christ. It's easy to keep Christ compartmentalized in a comfortable little corner: only intentionally living our lives in, through, with, and for Him during Mass, times of prayer, or during the times we engage in the works of mercy spelled out in the Sermon on the Mount. And yet, that isn't the kind of life we are being asked to live.

In 1 Corinthians 10:31, St. Paul drops the bomb that should be the cornerstone for every single thing we do in life: "Whatever you eat, then, or drink, and whatever else you do, do it all for the glory of God."

St. Paul is telling us that we are called to do everything for the glory of God, and using the gifts of creation God has handed down to us may be one of the most paramount of these opportunities. The questions is: How?

Dorothy Day provides the blueprint: "Love is the only solution."

If we work hard to do everything, most especially creating, in love, through love, with love, and for love, we will answer this radical call. God is love, and love is all we need

TOMMY TIGHE

Author of *The Catholic Hipster Handbook*
Host of *The Chimney* on Sirius XM's The Catholic Channel
catholichipster.com

GET OUT OF THE WAY

It seems the most profound things get created when we get out of the way. When we let go of control, intentions, plans, and give the Holy Spirit space to work and use us.

In my experience, whether I'm opening my mouth in front of a microphone or sitting down with an instrument to pray and write - when I truly get out of the way - God creates. Instrument builders often talk about how the pinnacle of their craft is to produce an instrument that essentially disappears in the hands of the musician; nothing should stand between the creator and the creation. So, get out of the way.

DANIEL HARMS

Musician and Speaker
danielharms.com

just put it on paper

CHRISTIE
VAUGHN

These are the words of my Grandfather, who I know mostly from stories. But it was his age-old advice – start somewhere, write it down, and let the idea begin.

Whether it's journaling, sketching, or painting, I always come back to this place of getting it on paper. My shelves are filled with countless sketchbooks that house my most interior thoughts and provide the opportunity to play and create. And that's where the magic happens - where the spark of an idea manifests on that empty page. To create is to risk, but it's so worth it. God won't leave you to flounder, but He also expects you to trust the process.

As an art teacher, I now incorporate this same mindset with my students. Whenever we start a new project, we come to the place of putting it down on paper – whether it's drawing up three thumbnail sketches or writing three sentences from a prompt. It has become an undeniable part of our classroom culture and I hope that my students adopt it as part of their own brainstorming process.

So maybe you don't know where to start?
Just put it on paper. Granddad knew best.

CHRISTIE PETERS

Artist and Teacher
Co-founder of Every Sacred Sunday
christievaughn.com

FIGHT
RESISTANCE
&
FIGHT HARD

You finally sit down to write that novel, and you suddenly wonder if the concept is stupid.

The night before you're going to perform a solo at church, your head is abuzz with visions of failure and humiliation.

This is Resistance. Bestselling author Steven Pressfield coined the term when he described Resistance as the force that "obstructs movement only from a lower sphere to a higher." It is the sinister force that opposes all creation.

Art is creative, in the most literal sense of the word. It brings life into the world. It humanizes us. It puts us in touch with God. And that's why it will always involve a fight.

Resistance wants only death, destruction, and nothingness. It wants you to quit. It wants you to listen to its whispers that you have no talent and your idea isn't that original and everyone is going to laugh at you anyway. It wants you to stay locked in the prison of your fear that your work isn't good enough. In the end, it wants you to leave this earth without having created a single thing.

And that is why you cannot – you must not – ever listen to Resistance.

JENNIFER FULWILER

Bestselling author and radio host
thejfshow.com

Burn
the
Plow

In the Book of First Kings, chapter 19, we first meet Elisha, working in the field. He's driving a plow pulled by twenty-four oxen. It's a job he's done many times. It's a job he's good at. But it's not what he was created to do. God had a much bigger plan for Elisha. Much bigger than fields of dirt. Much bigger than a couple dozen oxen. Much bigger than an old plow. He just didn't know it yet.

Enter Elijah.

Without saying a word, Elijah walks up to Elisha in the field and places his cloak on Elisha's dirty, sweaty shoulders. If we were standing in Elisha's muddy shoes, we might now have understood what Elijah was doing, but the significance and severity of that action was not lost on Elisha: Elijah – the most famous prophet in the world – was offering Elisha an incredible opportunity. He was calling Elisha to leave everything behind and follow him.

That day in the field, Elisha had two choices: (1) Stay with the plow and play it safe; or (2) leave everything behind and set off into the unknown to discover who God created him to be. Elisha chose option (3): slaughter the oxen, burn the plow, and then set off into the unknown. Elisha knew that if he was really going to find out who he was created to be, he needed to do it without a safety net.

What about you? Are you truly seeking who God created you to be, or are you playing it safe? As for me, I'm tired of playing it safe – in my art, my ministry, my life. I'm ready to go all in for the Gospel. I'm ready to burn the plow.

MICHAEL MARCHAND

Catholic Evangelist, Author, and Speaker
Co-founder of ProjectYM
projectym.com

Your art should drive you mad. It should drive you crazy. You should be regularly saying to yourself, "It's not good enough. I'm not good enough."

You should then balance this with saying "God, I've done what I can. I've given everything I had. It was the best I could do."

Of course, the question remains: Was it the best you could do? Or was it "good enough..."

There's plenty of originality in being an artist. But being original is hard: it means being different enough that the criticisms will come. And they'll hurt. Which means your only consolation will be God. And some days, He doesn't seem to be a fan.

The truth is, you're not good enough. And it isn't good enough. So you strive for perfection. But only God is perfect. Thus, your imperfect creation - and for that matter, imperfect self - will fall short. And that should drive you crazy.

LINO RULLI

Radio Host and Author
Host of *The Catholic Guy* show: Sirius XM Satellite Radio

During my high school years, my family suffered a myriad of difficulties and had to downsize our life—which meant packing eight of us into a very small house. Tensions were high to say the least. One day, I felt inspired to clear out a corner of the basement to make it into my own artist's studio. I painted on all the old stuff I could find. Painting fish and underwater scenes on glass vases, I found a safe place to pour out my heart. I had a real sense of God's presence in this space, and I would talk to the Lord about what was in my heart. The bright colors and whimsical scenes introduced something beautiful amid the messiness of my life in that moment. I have come to see this discovery of beauty amid pain as my own artistic process, which is gradually evolving as my relationship with Christ deepens.

When we don't see our weakness as a gift, we run from the messiness of our human experience and compensate by making our work saccharine, sterile, inauthentic, and devoid of the life that re-creation imbues. Good and true art needs to be lived with God. It is re-creative love which makes art truly beautiful. God is with you in the messiness. He is recreating in and through and with you in the messiness. Invite him in and stick around. Together, you will make beautiful things.

SISTER **DANIELLE VICTORIA LUSSIER**

Artist and Photographer
Daughters of St. Paul
@Danielleshabit on Twitter

AND STAY

"Jesus' death on the cross is arguably one the most pivotal moments in history. And like most crucial moments, it's important to look at who was there and why. Who do we see with Jesus as He died? His mother, Mary Magdalene, and John, the Beloved Disciple. Out of all of Jesus's followers, you have to wonder why it was just those few witnessing Christ's last moments. Quite simply, they showed up and stayed. When everyone, themselves included, was terrified and didn't feel like coming that morning, they still came.

Secondly, and this is just as important, they stayed. Things got very chaotic, scary, and brutal and they could have easily left. But they didn't. They stayed until the very end because they knew what was important.

I find this so important in creating. So often, the project seems too hard and overwhelming or I feel uncomfortable. It's crucial to not only show up but stay until it's done."

ROB KACZMARK

Filmmaker
spiritjuicestudios.com

It reawakens one's sense of wonder where one enters into the eternal "I AM" of God. When the heart encounters beauty, time ceases and only the present matters. The thought of forever can often bring a feeling of fear, entrapment, or boredom. But when one's heart, in an instant, is pierced by a glimpse of beauty, one does not want that particular moment to end, but rather the heart aches for that beauty to last forever – it pleads to go ever deeper into that one newly opened prism, because the heart knows there is no way one could ever fully exhaust the mystery. It keeps on giving and giving.

An encounter of beauty is one of discovery and learning – it never remains stale or static, but thrusts one forward into ever new surprise. Beauty opens a portal into the eschaton where we can behold in awe the One who is ever ancient, and ever new, one who is present with us now as the Eternal Present.

BROTHER DAVID BROKKE SOLT

Painter and Photographer
beautymakesallthingsnew.wordpress.com

YOUR WORD BE ——————————

PROPHETIC

"For he who is now called a prophet was formerly called a seer." 1 Samuel 9:9

The words of the prophet in Hebrew culture were the words of a seer. He first caught a divine image and had to transform it into words so that others could share in the vision.

Art is similar. Bad art belongs to those who are more concerned with being heard than they are with catching the vision. We rush to words out of fear and arrogance. Creativity is lacking because our sins obscure not our voice, but our vision, for the proud have no clue how to be receptive.

True art is the fruit of contemplative receptivity. You announce through the brush, plays, or podcast feeds what you were graced to see, no more or less. Creativity is that precarious space in between the seeing and the speaking, where you and the Word commingle in Spirit and in truth.

My word of caution to every artist: Be still and behold. Do not speak until you have first seen. To do otherwise makes you not just a bad artist, but a false prophet.

MICHAEL GORMLEY

Catholic Evangelist and Podcaster
Founder of Lay Evangelist | **layevangelist.com**
Co-host of Catching Foxes | **catchingfoxes.fm**

Art has the potential of tapping into something beyond the sum of its parts, to take the recipients beyond themselves to contemplate the human mystery. That place where we, and all before us, throw our questions to the stars and ask who are we, what are we, and where are we going. It has the ability to be a portal, an icon, to a room of true contemplation on these universal questions.

Art is not the answer to our questions, but in some way attached to it. If we allow it, we can feel the vibrations of the Creator's voice resonating towards us through it. If we open ourselves up to this potential, we can hear, if only for a moment, sound waves from the song of life plucked by the Creator's hand, like the low E string of an upright bass. If air, material, and vibration are the conduits of sound needed to hear that bass, then Beauty is the conduit of the Creator and art can be the language of Beauty.

Some art exists merely to celebrate the materials used and the hands that made it, rather than to reveal something greater of both. Art made in this way becomes an idol.
There is greater potential, which I prefer:
I want the mystery;
I want the conversation;
I want the icon.

MIKE MANGIONE

Musician
Mike Mangione and the Kin
mikemangione.com

REMEMBER YOUR DEATH

Art is so powerful it can be dangerous.

Created in the image of God, we touch both our identity and the truth of God—who is Beauty and the Creator of the Universe—through our creativity.

The natural introspection of creative souls inspires great art. But sensitive souls sometimes retreat so far within the ego that their creative action runs the risk of becoming a form of isolated self-approbation. Artists can also fall into the trap of creating merely to shock, amaze, get attention, and, ultimately, to magnify themselves rather than God. Because art is a powerful tool for both good and evil, artists have a great responsibility to unite their work with God.

The Latin phrase *memento mori,* or "Remember, you will die", is part of a long-standing Christian practice of remembering one's mortality in order to live well. Popular in medieval times, this practice has been lost in the popular imagination but it would be particularly beneficial to artists.

Life is short and heaven is our goal.

Remembering our death can help to center the artist's creative experience in God, who informs and gives unimaginable power to all we create

SISTER THERESA ALETHEIA NOBLE FSP

Writer
pursuedbytruth.com

Artists and architects are called to represent the Incarnation in their work. Through gratitude and awe of the mystery of the Incarnation, we strive to create more and more perfect images of God's likeness.

In some way, architecture should be anthropomorphic, based on man who is created in God's image, and on the Man-God in all His glory. This combination of the human and divine in architecture reflects the mystery of Christ's dual nature. Each church we build, then, is a new representation of the Incarnation; the church symbolizes Christ's body, with a focus on the head.

An architecture that reflects the Incarnation is one that rejects the ugliness of sin. It turns instead to beauty found in God's creation, and to mysteries both earthly and celestial. The Word became flesh and dwelt among us. Our task is to incarnate Christ's body in our art and architecture.

DUNCAN G. STROIK

Architect and Author
Founder of Duncan G. Stroik Architect, LLC
Professor at University of Notre Dame
stroik.com

God asks us to show up, just as we are. He asks me to show up as I uniquely am and to be influenced by my own experiences and share myself in my work. I interact with life, I enter fully into life and allow myself to be vulnerable to the happenings of life and then I have something to bring to my canvas. When I come at my design work genuinely and with all that I am, then I am bringing Christ into it.

He also asks us to show up every day - good days and bad days, to show up when there isn't a paid job on the table, to show up when we don't know where the next job will come from. I just have to create something, anything really. It is in those moments that the growth happens, where I can explore new avenues and try new techniques. Sometimes showing up to my paper even means that I go on a hike or I visit a museum where I can breathe and be inspired. But no matter what is going on in life, I must show up and once I am there, He sends me the work that I need to be able to buy groceries and pay rent. He delights in providing for us.

ERICA TIGHE

Calligrapher, Designer, and Author
Written by Hand
beaheart.com

Sentimentality, false optimism, feigned sincerity: these are all merely excuses by which we justify the worship of our own ego under the venerable title "art." Some of the time we can even fool others (and, if we're particularly benumbed, ourselves) into thinking that what we're doing is meaningful, that it isn't rooted in a twofold compulsion for validation and an inveterate fear of intimacy with others.

But our tragic hunger to be heard does not have the final word. There is another way; a messier, bloodier, freer way. A way expressed through the juxtaposition of the Virgin and the Prostitute beneath the outstretched arms of the man they both loved: one untouched and inviolate; the other familiar with every kind of touch on every inch of her body; both women alive in the hope of new life where there is less than nothing. A way that winds amongst the outcast, ugly, broken, scandalous, perverted, addicted: and not only touches but embraces these people and situations without seeking to cajole them into a conveniently sanitized trophy.

The true artist is the consummate realist: the one who remains awake, nerve-endings tingling (and wracked) with absorption. He is the one who gradually learns how to discern the Word- the meaning- in a world distressed by absurdity and noise. She is the one who possesses a genuine taste for that which is human, an insatiable urge to "be with." She desires to understand nakedness - to know, see, touch and taste the contours beneath the veil. To stand naked herself before the great Thou, unselfconscious but electrifyingly actualized, every pore open and waiting.

This is true artistry: to identify with the man who identified with mankind to the point of becoming physically unwrapped. It is to learn how to see the mystery others present to you, even in their foibles and inconsistencies- and to recognize yourself therein. Having a sacramental imagination doesn't consist of getting weak-kneed and weepy every time you see a bunny rabbit, or gasping "How beatific!" each time you behold lovers kissing. At heart, it means that when you look at a crucifix- whether in the church or in the cruciform body of your friend dying from cancer in his bed- what you see is God. God, gasping, dying, seeking, promising the "something more", the "almost, but not quite yet."

ALANNA BOUDREAU

Singer & Songwriter
alannaboudreaumusic.com

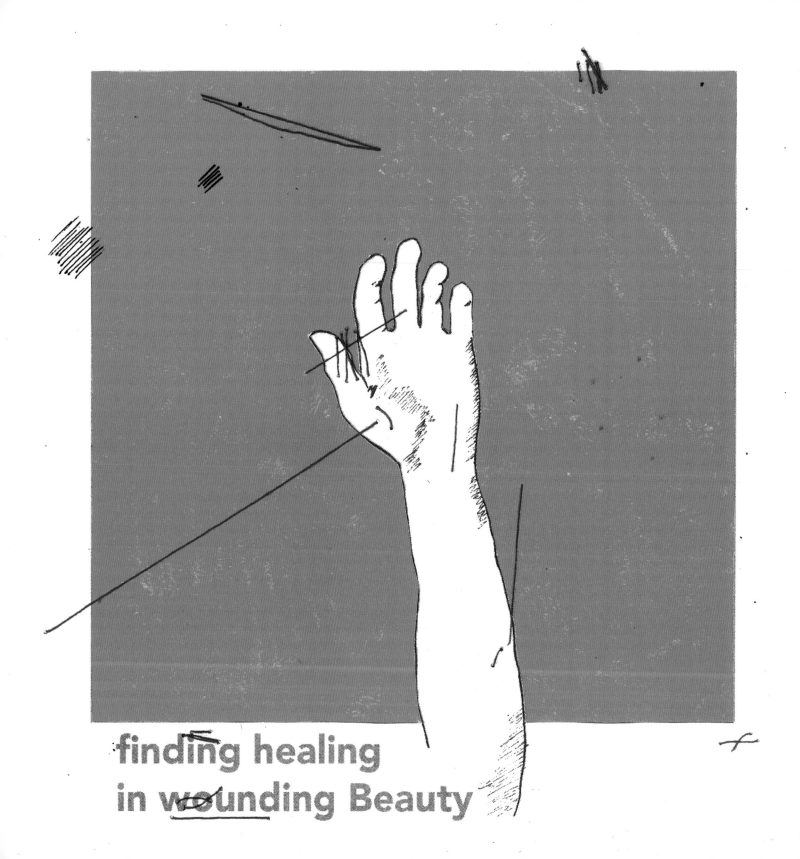

finding healing
in wounding Beauty

"True knowledge is being struck by the arrow of Beauty that wounds man... Being struck and overcome by the Beauty of Christ is a more real, more profound knowledge than mere rational deduction." - Joseph Ratzinger

"We no longer dare to believe in beauty and we make of it a mere appearance in order the more easily to dispose of it." - Hans Urs von Balthasar

The central truth Catholics profess is that Christ is Creator become creation, Wounded Healer, and the Resurrected One whose beauty the whole world longs to see.

When "beauty" has no conviction, no contradiction, no challenging qualities- when it comforts the afflicted but does not afflict the comfortable, it is a pale and empty version of what it could be. Worse, it implies that there is nothing under the veil- neither need for redemption nor healing to be found through our suffering. Is this the sort of art that people of faith should make? Or should the richness of our orthodoxy be embedded in our art?

Follow Christ. Let your wounds become a source of healing. Make beauty that is raised up for all to see because it has climbed the hill to Calvary.

WILLIAM PRICE, III

Filmmaker and Artist
Founder of Whiskey Ginger Please, Inc
whiskeygingerplease.com

God gifted us with creativity to make life an ever-abundant source of goodness. Life isn't a zero-sum game unless we make it so. But beyond that, everything we have, everything we do, everything we are, we owe it to Him. The only way we have to pay it back is to pay it forward.

With this perspective in mind, everything changes:
Another artist's success is something to celebrate, not envy.
Competition is a sign of opportunity in the field, not a threat.
Others' talent is a source of inspiration, not of insecurity.
Rejection is a chance to learn and improve, not to despair.
Newcomers deserve our advice, not our cold shoulder.

So let's rejoice in other's victories and even in our own trials, as both can make us grow. Our latest great idea, exciting project, and chance to shine are not the last we'll ever have.

Our God is a God of abundance, a God of hope: The harvest is plentiful but the workers are few, not the other way around.

DANIELA MADRIZ

Freelance Designer
danielamadriz.com

Permission to speak the unspoken.

Too often, truth is displaced in favor of being "nice" or "safe." Speaking the truth isn't always safe, but speaking the truth (nicely and out of love) is always necessary. Creative work usually calls for a personal investment of self, but when it comes to communicating that work, we're afraid of hurting someone's feelings or we're afraid to honestly share our thoughts in the process.

It's invaluable to be surrounded by people who challenge us to become better in our work and care enough to push for achieving greatness instead of settling for "good enough." This requires an intense level of vulnerability because speaking or accepting truth touches that deep place where authenticity lives. That's where the most original level of creativity can be found.

In creative circles, that kind of honest community is a blessing. Beauty, art, and creativity are all linked to truth. Taking "good enough" out of our vocabulary allows us to go the extra mile, challenge ourselves further, and become more authentically creative.

We hold ourselves to a higher standard, one that pushes through fear instead of skirting around the truth, by giving each other the permission to speak the unspoken.

GLASS CANVAS TEAM

glasscanvas.io

ARTWORK: GLASS CANVAS TEAM

What I'm going to say might sound extreme, but I say it because the Church I fell in love with was the bride arrayed in splendor, beautiful beyond measure, and I want to see her in all her radiance once again. The reality is that she is suffering from an ailment, a distortion that is as deep and scarring as Arianism or the Iconoclasts. The Church is sick with the lie that there is a division between the true and the beautiful. We see the symptoms of this sickness in every stained glass window purchased from a catalogue. We recognize its effects in all of the many conferences that emphasize "teaching the truth," but contain little experience of it. We hear its hacking cough every time a cacophonous choir strikes up the processional hymn on Sunday. The great tragedy is that we no longer see beauty as integral to expressing God's nature, instead it's just a thin veneer, it's a decoration. It's unnecessary, not worth the cost. God, save us from this unhappy utilitarianism!

Beauty is the very *conduit* by which truth is experienced; it is *inseparable* from truth. To deny this is to deny the heart of our faith. Ponder this for a moment; God desired that the invisible, spiritual reality of His being be reflected in a physical world where His image could be touched, heard, seen, felt. Beauty is who He is. He is not a disembodied truth but the truth *incarnate*. When St. Augustine writes that a sacrament is "an outward and visible sign of an inward and invisible grace," his words speak to the means by which God manifests Himself. How have His people come to see beauty as an afterthought? How has beauty become the first budget item we cross off the list at the end of the year? We've sacrificed beauty on the altar of utility, and in so doing have sacrificed God Himself. Are we truly worshiping *Him* when we cast beauty aside?

Next time we are faced with the question of whether or not to invest our time, our work, or our finances into beauty, I ask that you to consider this: When God faced the same question, did he spare any expense? How much did it cost him to take on human flesh? How much did it cost him to create you?

MARCELLINO D'AMBROSIO

Creative Director
Sherwood Fellows Creative Agency
sherwoodfellows.com

IN THE MIDST OF
Creation

"Let your religion be less of a theory and more of a love affair."
- G.K. Chesterton

We don't have to have it all figured out to come to Jesus with our lives. In the same way, we are free to approach the subject of religious art without the theories and concepts fully mapped out. When art and design is approached humbly with authenticity, there is room for the Holy Spirit to work. Just as falling in love rarely happens just as we plan, so creative breakthroughs are often found, not in the planning, but in the midst of creation. Trust in the guidance of God working through the object of your inspiration. Bring your gifts to Him – then get to work. As you strive to love God and glorify Him in your work, be confident that He will meet you in the middle of the mess.

In my time as a designer, I've often found it challenging to give good design advice. I struggle to come up with something unique and useful to offer. The truth is, there's no one formula or method that I use when I create. For me, to design is to experiment. Keep trying new things until you reach something that moves you. Ask the Holy Spirit to work through you and trust that He will.

CASSIE PEASE

Owner and Designer at Cassie Pease Designs
Creative Coordinator at Word on Fire
cassiepeasedesigns.com

Your ART is your PRAYER

When I was pregnant with my third son, I had a condition that caused me to itch incessantly. It filled me with anxiety, and left me feeling like a recluse who could not leave home lest I strip off all my clothes and itch myself to death! A pregnant recluse with two small rambunctious boys was not a recipe for a peaceful environment. People encouraged me to offer it up, but that felt so abstract, I didn't know where to begin.

I decided to take up watercoloring as a distraction. I taught myself how to put a brush to paper and pretend like I knew what I was doing, and I began hand lettering as well. I knew nothing about what I was doing, but when I painted and lettered, I no longer itched and my anxiety melted away.

The words I paint and the people I paint them for are my prayer, my offering to God. I think it's telling that in my weakest moments, I created something beautiful that has brought hope and beauty to others. It's a testament to what God can do in our littleness when we let our art, what we create, be our prayer.

MARIE HEIMANN

Watercolor Artist and Hand Letterist
fawnly.com

The
Mission
is Me

The Church is missionary by nature (*Ad Gentes*, 2). In my work in youth ministry and music ministry, I have tried to keep this close to my heart. In order to remain focused, I needed to remember this so as to not become complacent and content. For years I gave up time with family, friends and even leisure because I was accomplishing "God's will" for me. I spent hours and hours preparing for youth nights, bible studies, praise and worship events, and pouring into the lives of my volunteer core members. I was successful, mostly, but as months and years went on, I found myself running on an empty tank. I started to lose my passion- my drive-and the ministry began to suffer. What was wrong? I was giving myself to the "mission of the church" so why was this happening? After months of trying everything, I finally had to stop everything. In frustration and defeat, I turned to God with a heavy heart, a confused heart, an angry heart. Why was I not reaching teens? Why are my volunteers leaving? Why is my music not inspiring and touching hearts?

The answer was pretty simple. I had forgotten that Christ' mission is me. I had forgotten that Christ came to save and rescue me. He is working to convert my heart, not my ministry. He wanted my heart, not just my work. He wanted me. I am his mission. So I took time for silent prayer. I conversed with God in Eucharistic Adoration. I went to daily Mass as much as possible and I made family time a priority. These places are where God inspires us first. Coming to him in prayer, silence, and on the Sabbath is where we find the source of creativity and imagination.

Indeed, God gave us a mission but that mission is not just our work. You and I, as members of the Church, the Body of Christ, must remain missionary but we cannot forget that God sent his Son into the world for me and for the world. I am Christ's mission, my heart, my life, my work.

FRANCIS CABILDO

Singer and Songwriter
franciscabildomusic.com

PRAY

REFLECT

INVITE

God

INTO

YOUR

PROCESS

PERSEVERE

TRUST

CONNECT

Having worked as a designer for 15+ years, I had wanted to make Catholic art for a long time. It struck me one day as I was scrolling through a design blog how much darkness was glorified in my industry. I had to do something about it. I had to put my fears and insecurities aside and get to work. God was calling me to a mission. Was I going to say yes, or keep doing the comfortable thing, the easy thing?

God is calling each one of us to do His work, we know this. He wants and loves us so much and has such awesome things in store. As that impetus bubbles up inside of our hearts, prompting us to act, He is there, inspiring and guiding. The hardest part for me was, and still is, surrender and trust.

What does inviting God into your process look like? Realizing that your work is meant to be shared; that the world is thirsty for the light your creations can reflect. Inviting Him in means serving the truth with what you make. Inviting Him into your process is the absolute best place to start.

TRICIA DUGAT

Designer
providential.co

LET DOING COME FROM

BEING

My first album was five years in the making, written during some powerful transitions in my life: graduating college, getting a job, getting married, miscarrying our first child, and giving birth to our second. The music came from how I experienced the Lord during those times.

That album was successful. Wildly successful. So I sat down and tried to "do" a sequel. I wouldn't say the resulting CD was bad. There were certainly some good songs. But it had nowhere near the impact that the first one had. Looking back, I can see why: I was more interested in making a product than a prayer. St. John Paul II wrote, "Ours is a time of continual movement which often leads to restlessness, with the risk of 'doing for the sake of doing'. We must resist this temptation by trying 'to be' before trying 'to do'" (*Novo Millennio Ineunte*, 15).

As artists, what we do comes from who we are. A tree seeks nourishment from its roots, not from the fruit it creates. In the same way, we need to be rooted in our identity as sons and daughters of God, and let all we "do" flow from that.

DOCTOR **BOB RICE**

Professor at Franciscan University of Steubenville
bob-rice.com

Danny Jacobs requested that this page be left blank in order for you to reflect on this simple prayer.

DANNY JACOBS

Voice-over Artist
King Julien, *Madagasgar series*

BE
PRESENT
ASK
QUESTIONS
LOVE

During production of our first feature film, I was blessed to get to know our First Assistant Director, Dave. The 1st AD essentially runs the shoot. He's in charge. Every "Action!" call is his. Dave was tough, but clearly loved his job. He also espoused no particular faith background. I really liked Dave and asked if I could interview him for a behind-the-scenes video. He reluctantly agreed.

After we wrapped, I was packing-up gear and felt a tap on my shoulder. It was Dave. "Are you ready for that interview?" he asked. "Absolutely!" I responded. Dave described what the 1st AD does. After a minute, he paused to ask, "Should I refer to this as a Catholic thing or what?"

My response was whether you are Catholic, Evangelical, a non-believer, or whatever, our hope is that the viewer will relate to the humanity of the film, so "call it whatever you want."

He continued, "This is the first Catholic film I ever worked on." And he started to cry. After collecting his thoughts, he shared three things: "The script was beautiful. We became like a family producing it. And it really made faith accessible."

It is a joy and privilege for me to create artfully made, spiritually rich films. But they are a means to an end. The true call is in journeying with people– where they are– and encountering Christ together.

ERIC GROTH

Filmmaker
President/CEO of ODB Films
Executive Producer of *Full of Grace* and *Paul, Apostle of Christ*
odbfilms.com

BETTER HUMANS MAKE BETER ART

It's every photographer's dream to be able to work with a model who looks great from every angle, who is comfortable in front of the lens, and who knows how to pose his or her body. However, it is almost every photographer's reality that you are pointing your lens at people who do not believe they will look great from every angle, who feel uncomfortable face to face with a lens, and who have never felt more awkward in their bodies than they do in front of the camera.

The better, more virtuous artist doesn't lament this dilemma. Instead, being more in tune with the heart of God, they see not the imperfections that are skin-deep but the beauty shining forth from each soul. An artist who strives to be ever more kind, more charitable, more joyful... more Christ-like... that is the artist who can create work that illustrates the goodness of the world, and of each human being.

Growing in virtue is not an isolated pursuit separate from our art. It is a necessary qualification for becoming a better artist. As I work on my relationship with Christ and get to know His heart, He empowers me to bring peace, joy, and laughter on to every photo shoot so I can help others feel beautiful and see for themselves the beauty I see in them. Better people make better artists.

CHRISTINA MEAD

Author and Photographer
More Than a Pretty Face, That One Girl
christinamead.com

 I've always been inspired by artists who are "real" and vulnerable.

Their art has impacted me not only because it is raw and honest but also because it taps into the human desire that longs to have courage enough to face reality in all of its discomforts. These artists do not shy away from peacefully sharing with others what is fragile, weak and even crucified in their life, not to self-deprecate, but rather to communicate the journey through those places. The art becomes a unique window and lens through which the artist beckons "Come see what I've seen. Come feel what I've felt." The artist is a forerunner who invites others out on the path where he has already trodden, proposing "You too are not alone. You too can find hope. You too can find healing."

Artists remind and teach us what it is to be human. A heart that is vulnerable is more human because it is more disposed to love and be loved. I think this is what makes those who are "real" so attractive: they portray a fully human life, which requires one to be vulnerable. We need good art that is vulnerable to dispose other hearts to the Way that leads to Love.

JOE ZAMBON

Musician
joezambonmusic.com

PROVBS
PROEBS

HATERS GONNA HATE

9:8

I worked for several weeks on my debut rap song. I handpicked the beat. I had the wittiest word play ever. After it was perfect in every way, I emailed it to my favorite rapper. I anticipated wonderful affirmation. My song was not just great, it was revolutionary. Finally, a reply. I opened it.

"Don't rap."

Processing this joke, I waited for the follow up—you know, the real reply. It never came. After a childhood of praise, school days filled with awards, and a career advanced on artistic ability, "Don't rap" is the exact feedback I needed. It taught me I didn't have to choose between being confident and being humble—rather, the ability to accept criticism with humility was the test of authentic confidence. It took me years to acquire skills, and even longer to embrace those skills being challenged.

This attitude adjustment was invaluable with running an online community at phatmass.com, producing music with other artists and also in my own career. Instead of avoiding the haters, I learned to seek them to love them. Criticism is our blueprint towards perfection—an unattainable goal we should never give up on.

DUST SIEBER

Designer
Phounder of Phatmass.com
phatmass.com | catholic.hiphop

LISTEN
TO THEIR
HUNGER PAINS

When I lived in Italy, after a meal, the host would inevitably ask "How did you like your meal?" If I were to say, "I'm so stuffed", they would take that as an insult, a suggestion that they were overzealous in providing for me. Instead, I would give the traditional compliment "io sono contento"- *I am content*- to let the host know that his meal had left my deepest culinary yearnings satisfied.

A good meal is always prepared with the guest in mind. It's well-plated and bite-sized, so when you spread the table, your guest can't wait to say grace. It's also delicious, with flavors and sensations delicately balanced, matching exactly what the guest is hungering for. And finally, a good meal brings contentment, a warm feeling of well-being.

Just so, the faith is a feast and it's our job to present it. We have to plate it in the midst of a Christian life fully lived and make it bite-sized, just as Jesus ame not in the form of a giant, but of a tiny baby. We also have to make it elicious and balanced, answering the deepest longings of our fellow man. In his way, we make art that feeds souls, so that our guests will know the contentment that comes from having feasted at His table.

FATHER **LEO PATALINGHUG**

TV and Radio Host, Author, and Speaker
Founder and Creator of Grace Before Meals
gracebeforemeals.com

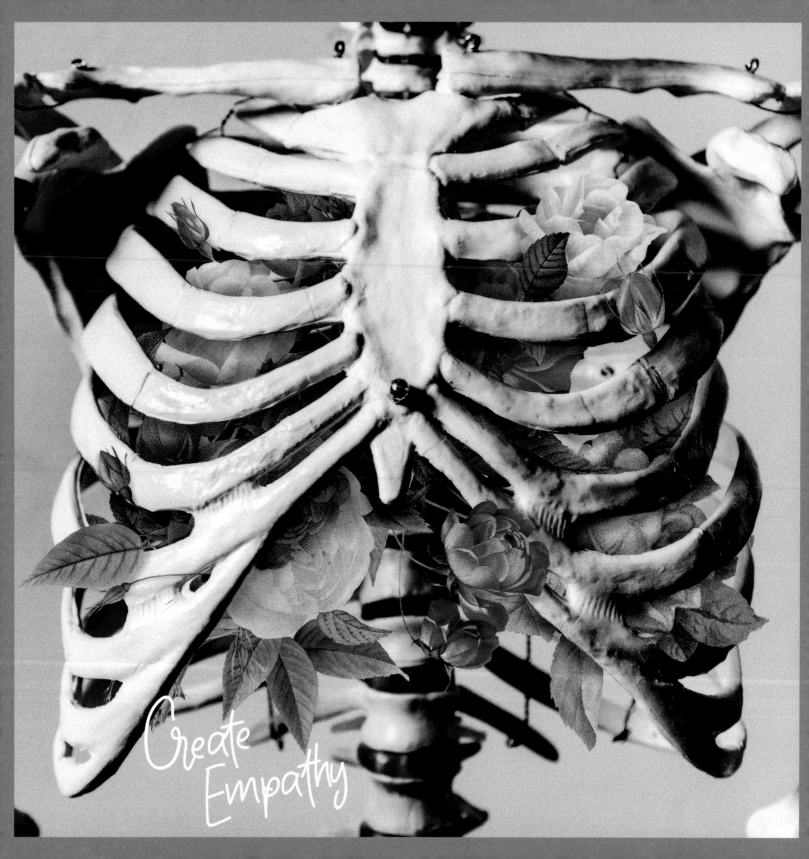

Create
Empathy

 The legendary acting/directing teacher, Judith Weston, once told me our impulse to create often comes from one of two life experiences: either an experience of great permission from our parents/teachers or from an experience of deep, dark, personal tragedy.

When art really moves us, we almost immediately recognize in our own unique experience, that sacred space from which the artist creates. We feel: "Oh yeah, I know that dark place" or "Oh Wow! I know how mind-blowingly beautiful that really is". Empathy is this after-effect of the artist baring their suffering, fears, joys, or pure bliss - truthfully in their work. It has the power to create a spiritual connection, to heal and make us all feel a lot less lonely.

Propagandists abuse the power of art and empathy to sell an agenda (or a luxury vehicle). Christian artists should rethink how we come to our respective canvases. We need to stop coming as the privileged truth bearers ready to save the world through fancy typeface or divinely-inspired design. Instead, we should approach the blank page as a confession; a brutally honest confession of our brokenness. Let it spill out, ugly and unfiltered; bleeding onto the page, the painting, the photograph, so others can recognize themselves.

Great art is an experience, shared. If empathy is defined as "the ability to understand and share in the feelings of others", then one could argue that God becoming human was the ultimate act of empathy.

Create empathy.

CHARLES FRANCIS KINNANE

Film Director
The Human Experience, Child 31, Saving Bill Murray
kinnanefilms.com

WINNING
THE
QUESTION

We all long to be seen by another. To be understood and known.

No one likes to be "talked at".

I think good art and good evangelization have this in common where you somehow feel mysteriously known. A friend of mine converted to Catholicism when he realized that the Church knew his questions better than he did. I don't think art and evangelization are primarily about winning an argument. They are about winning the question.

I recall a story about a man who was sitting outside at a cafe in a foreign country when he heard someone singing in the town square. He suddenly recognized the song as one that his mother and father used to sing to him as a child. There, on the other side of the world in a place he'd never been before, he was brought to tears because he was suddenly brought home. Art and the Faith devastate me with such experiences all the time.

Eden is the home we've lost and Heaven is the home we dare to hope for. We can't really see past these two horizons but we're all haunted by them, aren't we? If this hauntedness deep inside of us goes unacknowledged, I think we go mad or fall into despair. What do I grieve for? What do I hope for? Artists are called to reverently touch our deepest questions. This is a work of mercy. Art and beauty allow us to glimpse behind the veiled horizons of this valley of tears. Artists can help us remember home, help us grieve for Eden and groan for Heaven, sometimes in the same breath. This is why the scent of a used bookstore and the dimmed lights of a theater can feel like church to me.

DAVE KANG

Filmmaker
Writer, Producer, and Director of *The Humanum Series*
eccefilms.com

Creativity is woven into us.

My whole life, I was frustrated because I wasn't creative. I remember feeling discouraged in how I was formed, obviously made without a trace of creativity, void of all artistry and imagination.

And then a ministry, Blessed is She, was born.

For the first time, I grew. Not out of my own skills, but out of an openness to let the Lord move in me. I realized for the first time in my life that creativity was woven into my very being. I was becoming the very person God made me to be. The stretching caused my very bones and skin to grow, revealing the pieces of me I had never seen before. There, in my very soul, was woven a beautiful tapestry of a human. I was created for this growth, for this becoming, for this moment.

No longer in a mindset of victimhood to my uncreative life, I became alive in the work He made me for. I allowed the woven tapestry of my existence to finally be set free.

And you. You too.

You are not the person you were yesterday, if you choose it. If you choose the stretching, the learning, the growing. If you allow Him in. If you allow Him to move.

You and I will transform into the very humans God made us to be, with creativity woven into our very bones.

JENNA GUIZAR

Creative Director
Blessed is She
blessedisshe.net

present
christmas
irresistible

"I had just pinched all my pennies together and bought my first real camera. I was about to finish up college and it was time to finally have something I could call my own. It wasn't the best but it was mine and it was incredibly freeing to create whenever and whatever I wanted. My friend Tyler and I would go out on photography adventures and teach each other whatever we were learning. When he saw I didn't have a camera bag since I was as broke as they come, he offered me his and told me not to worry about it.

After graduation, I headed up to Michigan to marry my college sweetheart and start telling stories under the name Likable Art. Tyler graduated as well and came up to our wedding to wish us well and headed down to his home in Texas to pack up for a year documenting and filming in Malawi, Africa.

My wife and I had just gotten back from our honeymoon and I was working in the spare bedroom when I heard her gasp. Tyler had passed away during a bike ride from heart failure just days before flying to Africa. Feeling helpless, I pulled up his website. One thing stood out to me; he had written: "If I were to have a mission, I would assume it goes as follows: To present Christ, Christ as irresistible to the yearning heart."

That camera bag would come with me to shoots from Zambia to Haiti; it even found its way back after I accidentally left it in the middle of Manhattan. But what will live much longer than this camera bag is this mission that I have adopted from Tyler as my own: if Christ is who we say He is, then He is irresistible and longed for by every human heart.

CORY HEIMANN

Creative Director at Likable Art
likableart.com

FIND HIM IN THE CREATING

> We are made to create like God creates, in His image of creation. And that act of creating wasn't tainted by some delusion of Grandeur. He had all the Grandeur. That act of creation was created as gift. Pure gift. Here...all this is yours. Enjoy the raw materials. I made them for you.

From the essential Artist Himself, comes a playground for bonding oneself to the divine. Bust out the paints! Bust out the crayons! Bust out the glue sticks, the kind that starts purple and then dries invisible. The King has woven Himself in all of creation, seamless, only to have us poke our fingers through the cloth, ripping it in two, and find ourselves navel gazing in the absence of the garden. Not sure what to do with all this gift that we've received. Incapable of making the perfection that we see in the creation of raw materials before us. Not yet the masters of this domain.

We make things poorly, but we make them. And there's this spark of the Spirit that ignites our own creations. Regardless of what we're creating, we can find God in the fire, dancing. When you look at a piece of art, you can find Him in the created. But as an Artist, you're invited to find Him in the Creating.

ANDY BONJOUR

Professor at Franciscan University of Steubenville
andybonjour.com

Authentic art requires courage. The best art wells up from a place deep inside us inspired by a spark of the Holy Spirit. Its beauty reveals something deeply true about our humanity and our relationship to the divine. To express such depth requires an uncommon sincerity and vulnerability.

When I have taken leaps of faith, such as supporting my husband to pursue his vocation or opening an art shop or deciding to move across the country weeks before welcoming our fourth child or any time I sit with a paintbrush in hand, I imagine St. Peter's courageous step out of the boat into the tumultuous waves of a raging storm. Peter was not fearless as he walked out into the sea, but he remained determined to follow Jesus. Fulfilling our potential as artists requires a *fiat* of sorts - placing our talents into the outstretched hands of Jesus. Peter also reminds us of our dependence on grace. If we lose sight of our *telos* for even a moment, we will fall.

Dante Alighieri imagines God as "L'amor che move il sole e l'altre stelle"—*the love that moves the sun and the other stars.* Our cooperation in the divine act of creation means abandoning control and participating in this divine love. This is true at baptism when we choose to be reborn in Christ and conformed to His will. It is true as artists when we have the courage to attempt to let God's love speak through our talents in even the smallest of ways.

Walk on water with your art.

KATRINA HARRINGTON

Artist
roseharrington.com

A five-year-old girl was watching a classic animated movie, Walt Disney's Snow White and the Seven Dwarves. She had watched it many times, over and over again. Suddenly, the dancing images on the screen filled her with wonder and she thought, "God really must exist!". That little girl was me many years ago. And perhaps I don't remember this moment in exact detail, but the point is this encounter with a "magical" story awakened my soul and revealed the reality of a loving God.

Many Christians artists that I've spoken to go through a period of crisis when they don't know if they should use their creative talents in religious settings or in the "frivolous" secular world. I'm all for amazing religious art. Our Church needs it, badly. But I also know that God's grace is not confined by the boundaries of a church building and neither is His art. The Spirit works through all that is good, and good art is found everywhere. No matter where our creativity leads us, if our work unveils God's wonder to at least one person we have done our job well. It might even be someone's first step toward the eternal.

FABIOLA GARZA

Illustrator, Author, and Artist
Character Artist at Disney Creative Group
fabiolagarza.com

Don't worry.
You belong here.

 I used to have a corner in my apartment where I kept my paintings. They faced the wall, out of sight and out of mind. Some were professional work that'd been awarded; some were personal projects, meant to expand myskillset or to give me joy. None of them, though- to my mind, anyway- deserved to be seen. I was embarrassed by them. Their quality, I feared, didn't hold up to the work of artists I admired. The work wasn't good enough, so I wasn't good enough.

I'd wager that we all experience this kind of anxiety. Maybe it's about our craft; maybe it's about our own bodies. But the imposter syndrome that comes with being an artist – and moreover, being a person – is real. And yet, here's the thing: we're not called to re-create someone else's beauty. We're merely called to perfect our own.

We're called to be as the Biblical Magi, each bringing a different gift to the feat of our Lord. One gifting gold shouldn't compare himself to one gifting frankincense, nor either of them to the one gifting myrrh. We, like the Magi, are each called to bring our own personal form of beauty to He who gave it to us in the first place, recognizing that we belong before Him just like every artist and every child of God since time began. You are enough. Your beauty is enough. And the artists and thinkers featured in these pages are not your competition nor your betters; we are your brothers and sisters.

JACOB POPČAK

Illustrator and Designer
jacobpopcak.com

CREATE YOUR OWN FIVE WORDS

This book is for you and by you - it's your turn to contribute.

Take a minute to reflect on your first five words. Draw, design, collage, or macaroni your first five words on the left side. On the right side break down your five words in a few paragraphs.

Share on social media with the hashtag **#CreatedBook** and read the rest of the submissions.

THANK YOU SO MUCH

This book began as nothing more than an idea over two years ago. Many people worked very hard to form it into the piece of art you now hold in your hands. This book is about a lot of things, but one of its themes is celebrating the successes of other artists and those who support them. Indulge me, as I take a moment to do just that.

KUDOS

MARIE HEIMANN
My Wife and Greatest Collaborator, for being supportive every step of the way. Without you, this book wouldn't exist.

KYLE HEIMANN
The Wall At Which All Was Thrown To See What Sticks, for listening to me overthink every detail. This included everything from parsing through 200 title ideas in a 14-seat diner to agonizing over the ideal paper weight.

MARK GUINEY
Crowdfunder Extraordinaire and Editor. He tackled the giant that is Kickstarter, learning the ins and outs of running a fantastic campaign. Spelling is my kryptonite and his superpower. Find Mark at radioheartmedia.com

MAGGIE BONAR
Spreadsheet Wrangler and Logistics Czar. She took this project past the finish line, working for too many hours for too little pay. Google Docs cower in fear before her.

MICHELLE MARQUELING
Layout Queen and Design Authority. She whipped together the pages, kept chaos at bay, and answered our many questions. Visit Michelle at michellemarqueling.com

OLIVA BRATTON
Midnight Hero. She uncovered sources and double-checked facts. Most importantly, she helped find the narrative of this book. Meet Olivia at oliviabratton.wordpress.com

STEVEN JAGLA
Gracious Host. In a tough moment, he opened his home to us. He gave us a place to work on this book and helped keep us on a roll.

STEPHANIE JOHNSON
Money Maven. She kept track of every dollar and every order. Without her, we would broke and bookless.

RECOGNITION PATRONS

Andrew Montpetit

Will Hickl

SoulCore

Bob & Claire Keith

The Culture Project International

Mark J. Vojas, Jr.

Sean Allen

Brandon Vogt

Fabiola Garza

James and JoAnn Heimann

Kim DiBiase

Jp Talty

Joy Heimann

CONTRIBUTORS & ARTISTS

And, of course, a massive thank you to all of our amazing contributors-- these are are some fantastic people. We asked them to inspire, instruct, and illuminate, while limiting them to only 250 words and they certainly delivered! They have been tirelessly patient with us through email chains, art requests, and dozens of the other little details it takes to make a project like this come together.

INDEX OF ARTISTS

REFERENCES

p. 7
T. S. Eliot. *Burnt Norton* from The Four Quartets. San Diego, CA: Harcourt. 1943.

p. 7
Akira Kurosawa. *Something Like An Autobiography.* New York, NY: Vintage. 1983.

p. 9, 17, 29
St. John Paul II. "Letter to Artists." Vatican: the Holy See. Rome, Apr 1999. Web.

p. 9
St. Augustine of Hippo. *Confessions.* early 5th century.

p. 17
Fyodor Dostoyevsky. *The Idiot.* 1869.

p. 21
Flannery O'Connor Fitzegerald, Sally, ed.. A letter written 14 Nov 1959 from *A Habit of Being: Letters from Flannery O'Connor.* New York, NY: Farrar, Straus, and Giroux. 1979

p. 21
Pope Benedict XVI. "Address to the German pilgrims gathered in Rome for the inauguration ceremony of the Pontificate", Rome. April 2005. Web.

p. 39
Dorothy Sayers. "Why Work?" from *Letters to a Diminished Church: Passionate Arguments for the Relevance of Christians Doctrine.* Nashville, TN: Thomas Nelson. 2004.

p. 41
found in James Martin. *Essential Writings.* Ossining, NY: Orbis Books. 2017.

p. 49
Dorothy Day. *House of Hospitality.* New York, NY: Sheed and Ward. 1939.

p. 55
Steven Pressfield. *The War of Art.* New York, NY: Warner Books. 2002.

p. 79
Cardinal Joseph Ratzinger. "The Feeling of Things the Contemplation of Beauty." Rimini, Communion and Liberation (CL) meeting, Aug 2002. Web.

p. 79
Hans Urs von Balthasar. *Seeing the Form.* Edinburgh, United Kingdom: A&C Black. 1982.

p. 85
St. Augustine of Hippo. *Doctrinal Treatises.* 5th century.

p. 87
G. K. Chesterton. *St. Francis of Assisi.* London, United Kingdom: Hodder and Stoughton. 1923.

p. 91
Pope Paul VI. "Decree on the Missionary Activity of the Church - Ad Gentes." Vatican: the Holy See. Rome, Dec 1965. Print.

p. 95
St. John Paul II. "Apostolic Letter, Novo Millennio Ineunte." Vatican: the Holy See. Rome, Jan 2001. Web.

p. 119
Dante Alighieri. *The Paradiso.* early 14th century.